Killer Snakes

Egyptian Cobra

By Jessica O'Donnell

Gareth Stevens Publishing

Please visit our website, www.garethstevens.com. For a free color catalog of all our high-quality books, call toll free 1-800-542-2595 or fax 1-877-542-2596.

Library of Congress Cataloging-in-Publication Data

O'Donnell, Jessica.
Egyptian cobra / Jessica O'Donnell.
p. cm. — (Killer snakes)
Includes index.
ISBN 978-1-4339-5645-4 (pbk.)
ISBN 978-1-4339-5646-1 (6-pack)
ISBN 978-1-4339-5643-0 (library binding)
1. Egyptian cobra—Juvenile literature. I. Title.
QL666.O64O36 2011
597.96'42—dc22

2010053827

First Edition

Published in 2012 by
Gareth Stevens Publishing
111 East 14th Street, Suite 349
New York, NY 10003

Designer: Michael J. Flynn
Editor: Greg Roza

Photo credits: Cover, p. 1 Heinrich Van Den Berg/Gallo Images/Getty Images; (pp. 2–6, 8, 10, 12–16, 18, 20–24 snake skin texture), pp. 5, 7, 13, 19, 21 Shutterstock.com; p. 9 iStockphoto.com; p. 11 Ronald Toms/Oxford Scientific/Getty Images; pp. 14–15 Frank Greenway/Dorling Kindersley/Getty Images; p. 17 Gallo Images-Denny Allen/Riser/Getty Images.

Printed in the United States of America

CPSIA compliance information: Batch #CS11GS: For further information contact Gareth Stevens, New York, New York at 1-800-542-2595.

Contents

Boldface words appear in the glossary.

An Angry Snake

The Egyptian cobra is one of the most common snakes in Africa. It also lives on the Arabian **Peninsula**. The Egyptian cobra gets angry very easily. It makes a deadly **venom** in its body. Just one bite has enough venom to kill a person.

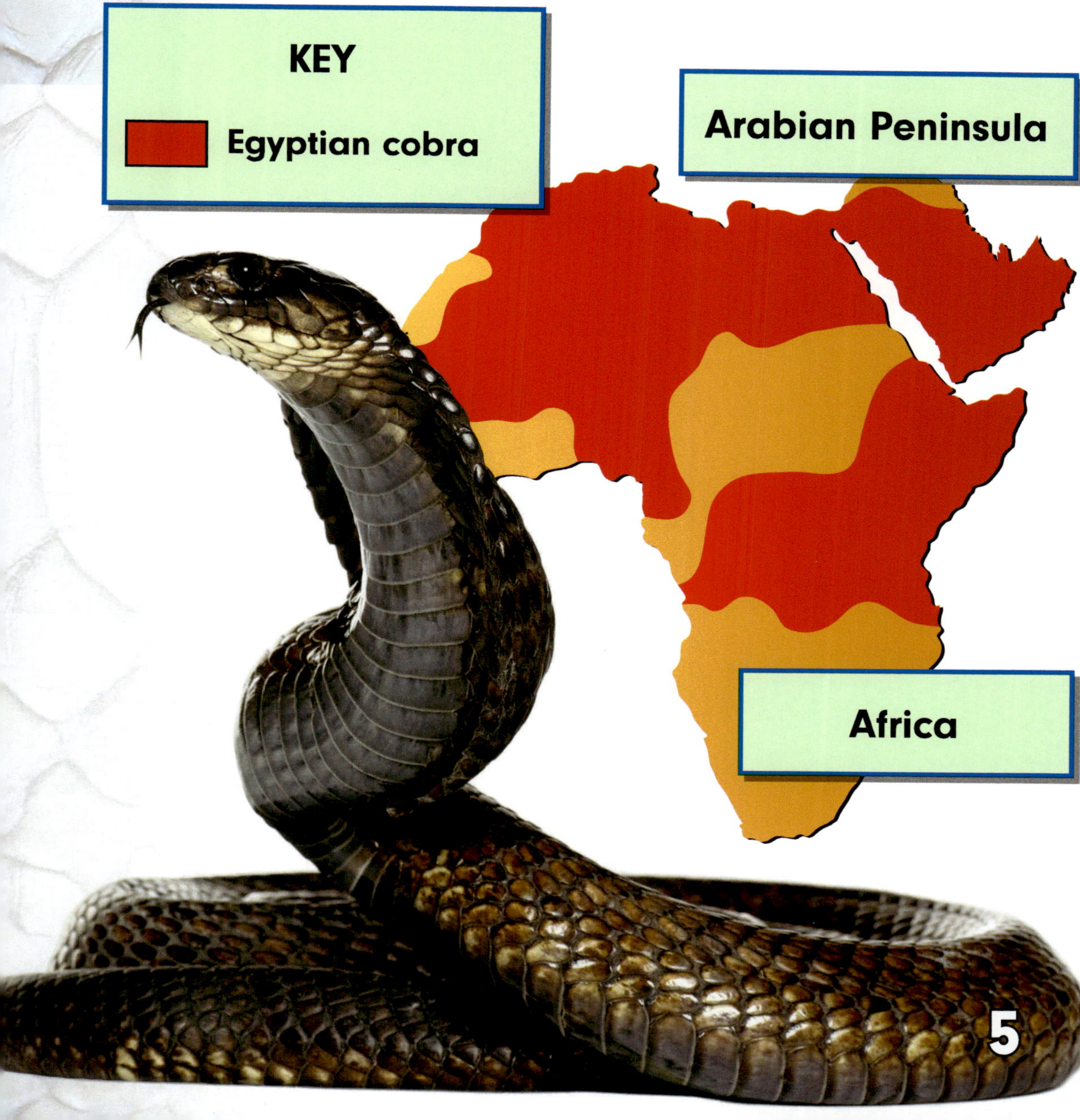
KEY
Egyptian cobra
Arabian Peninsula
Africa

Snake History

The Egyptian cobra was an important figure in Egypt long ago. Egyptian rulers wore crowns with a figure of an Egyptian cobra on them. They believed the cobra kept them safe. This snake was also a **symbol** for the sun.

At Home with Egyptian Cobras

Egyptian cobras live in hot places that have water. They live in grasslands, forests, and **oases**. They're often found near people's homes. Egyptian cobras may even enter a person's home while looking for a meal!

What Does It Look Like?

Adult Egyptian cobras are between 5 and 8 feet (1.5 and 2.4 m) long. They have thick bodies and thin tails. They're usually dark brown with light brown spots. Most have a dark band of color just below their head.

Cobra Hood

Like all cobras, the Egyptian cobra has a hood. When the snake wants to look larger and scarier, it raises the front half of its body off the ground. Then it makes the part of its body right below its head flatter and wider. The snake looks like it's wearing a hood.

Cobra Venom

The Egyptian cobra uses its **fangs** to shoot venom into an animal. Soon after being bitten, the animal can't move or breathe. The animal dies within about 15 minutes. People bitten by an Egyptian cobra need to take a drug called antivenin right away.

Time to Eat

Egyptian cobras hunt mainly at night. They eat many kinds of small animals, including mice, rats, frogs, toads, birds, and lizards. They eat other snakes, too. Egyptian cobras that live near people may even eat out of trash cans.

Stay Away!

An Egyptian cobra will **attack** when it's surprised or cornered. When in danger, it makes a loud hissing noise. The snake sways back and forth when its enemy moves. When the cobra strikes, it bites several times very quickly.

Egyptian Cobras and People

Egyptian cobras are often found near towns, cities, and farms. **Snake charmers** commonly use them for their acts because the cobras look like they're swaying to the music. Most bites happen to snake charmers.

Snake Facts
Egyptian cobra

Length	5 to 8 feet (1.5 to 2.4 m)
Color	shades of brown
Where It Lives	Africa, the Arabian Peninsula
What It Eats	many kinds of small animals, including other snakes
Killer Fact	Stories tell that the great Egyptian queen Cleopatra killed herself by letting an "asp" bite her. Many historians believe the asp was really the Egyptian cobra.

Glossary

attack: to try to hurt someone or something

fang: a long, sharp tooth

oases: wet, green places in the middle of a desert. The singular is oasis.

peninsula: a piece of land surrounded by water on three sides

snake charmer: someone who handles and dances with snakes to music

symbol: a sign that stands for something else

venom: something a snake makes in its body that can harm other animals

For More Information

Books

Johnson, Sylvia A. *Cobras.* Minneapolis, MN: Lerner Publications, 2007.

Kopp, Megan. *Cobras.* Mankato, MN: Capstone Press, 2011.

Riehecky, Janet. *Cobras: On the Hunt.* Mankato, MN: Capstone Press, 2009.

Websites

The Crocodile Hunter Diaries

animal.discovery.com/videos/the-crocodile-hunter-diaries-egyptian-cobra.html

Watch a short video of an Egyptian cobra ready to attack.

Egyptian Cobra

www.rfadventures.com/egyptian_cobra.htm

Read more about the Egyptian cobra.

Publisher's note to educators and parents: Our editors have carefully reviewed these websites to ensure that they are suitable for students. Many websites change frequently, however, and we cannot guarantee that a site's future contents will continue to meet our high standards of quality and educational value. Be advised that students should be closely supervised whenever they access the Internet.

Index